AF270613

AIDS CRISIS

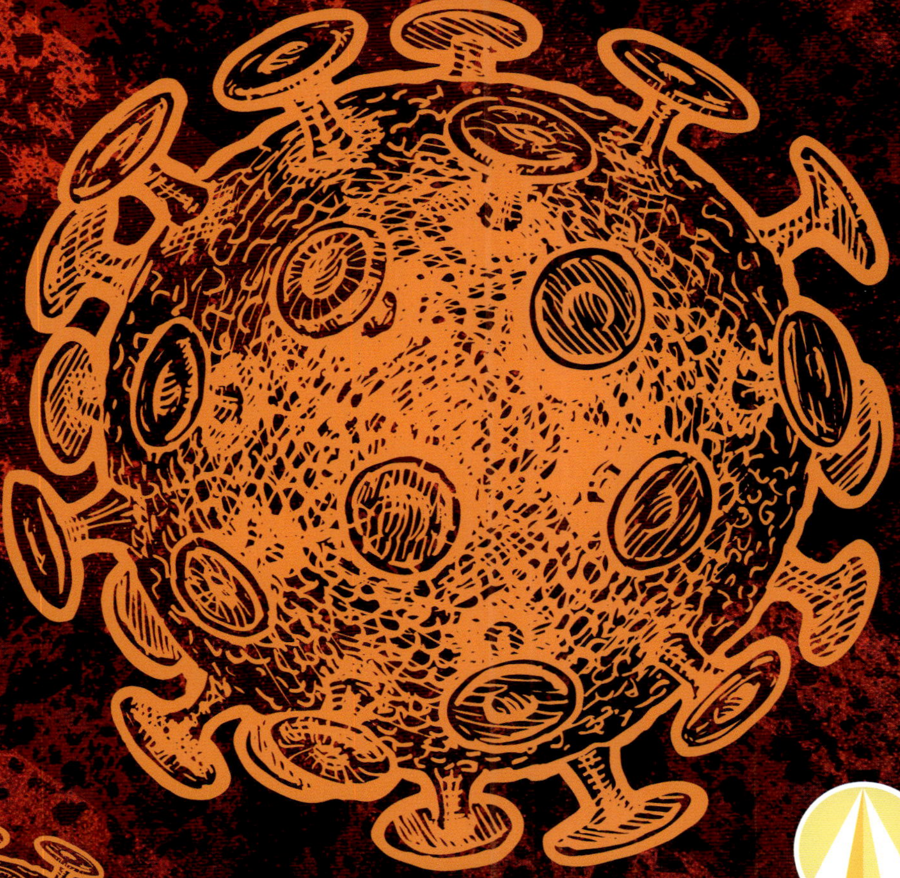

KENNY ABDO

abdobooks.com

Published by Abdo Zoom, a division of ABDO, P.O. Box 398166, Minneapolis, Minnesota 55439. Copyright © 2021 by Abdo Consulting Group, Inc. International copyrights reserved in all countries. No part of this book may be reproduced in any form without written permission from the publisher. Fly!™ is a trademark and logo of Abdo Zoom.

Printed in the United States of America, North Mankato, Minnesota.
102020
012021

Photo Credits: Alamy, AP Images, Granger Collection, Science Source, Shutterstock
Production Contributors: Kenny Abdo, Jennie Forsberg, Grace Hansen
Design Contributors: Dorothy Toth, Neil Klinepier, Laura Graphenteen

Library of Congress Control Number: 2020910920

Publisher's Cataloging-in-Publication Data

Names: Abdo, Kenny, author.
Title: AIDS crisis / by Kenny Abdo
Description: Minneapolis, Minnesota : Abdo Zoom, 2021 | Series: Outbreak! | Includes online resources and index.
Identifiers: ISBN 9781098223250 (lib. bdg.) | ISBN 9781098223953 (ebook) | ISBN 9781098224301 (Read-to-Me ebook)
Subjects: LCSH: AIDS (Disease)--Juvenile literature. | Immunodeficiency--Juvenile literature. | Epidemics--Juvenile literature. | Epidemics--History--Juvenile literature. | Plague--History--Juvenile literature.
Classification: DDC 614.49--dc23

TABLE OF CONTENTS

AIDS CRISIS

Silently infecting the masses, AIDS spread fear and death throughout the world.

NEW YORK POST
AIDS FUROR
FINAL
FOR THE MARATHON WATCHER
RACING
All you need to know about the city's 16th annual race
NEWS
Saturday, October 26
AIDS
NAISBITT: MEGATRENDS MAN
Newsweek
THE FEAR OF AIDS
Ignorance and Uncertainty Fuel
Growing Public Concern
1985 / $1.95
6

AIDS devastated many communities throughout the 1980s and 90s.

SYMPTOMS

Symptoms of AIDS include rapid weight loss and body sores. It can also cause fever, extreme tiredness, and memory loss.

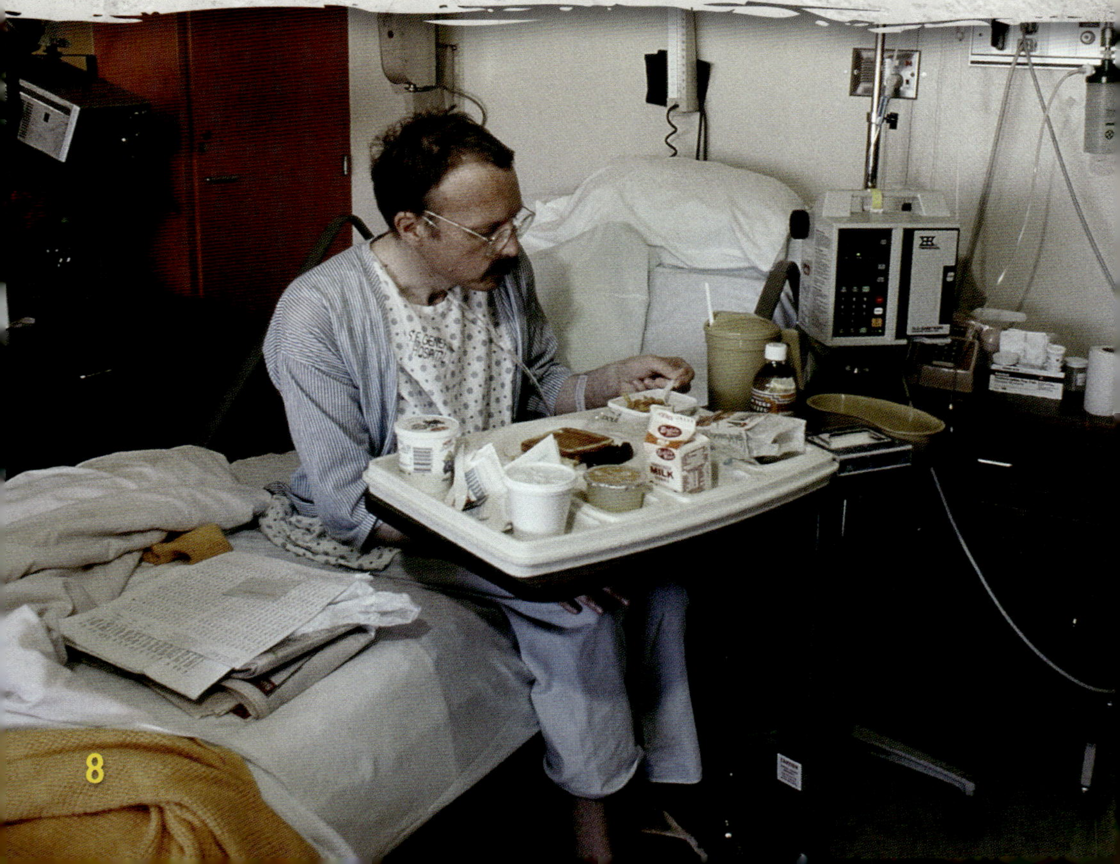

If left untreated, AIDS will eventually lead to death.

SOURCE

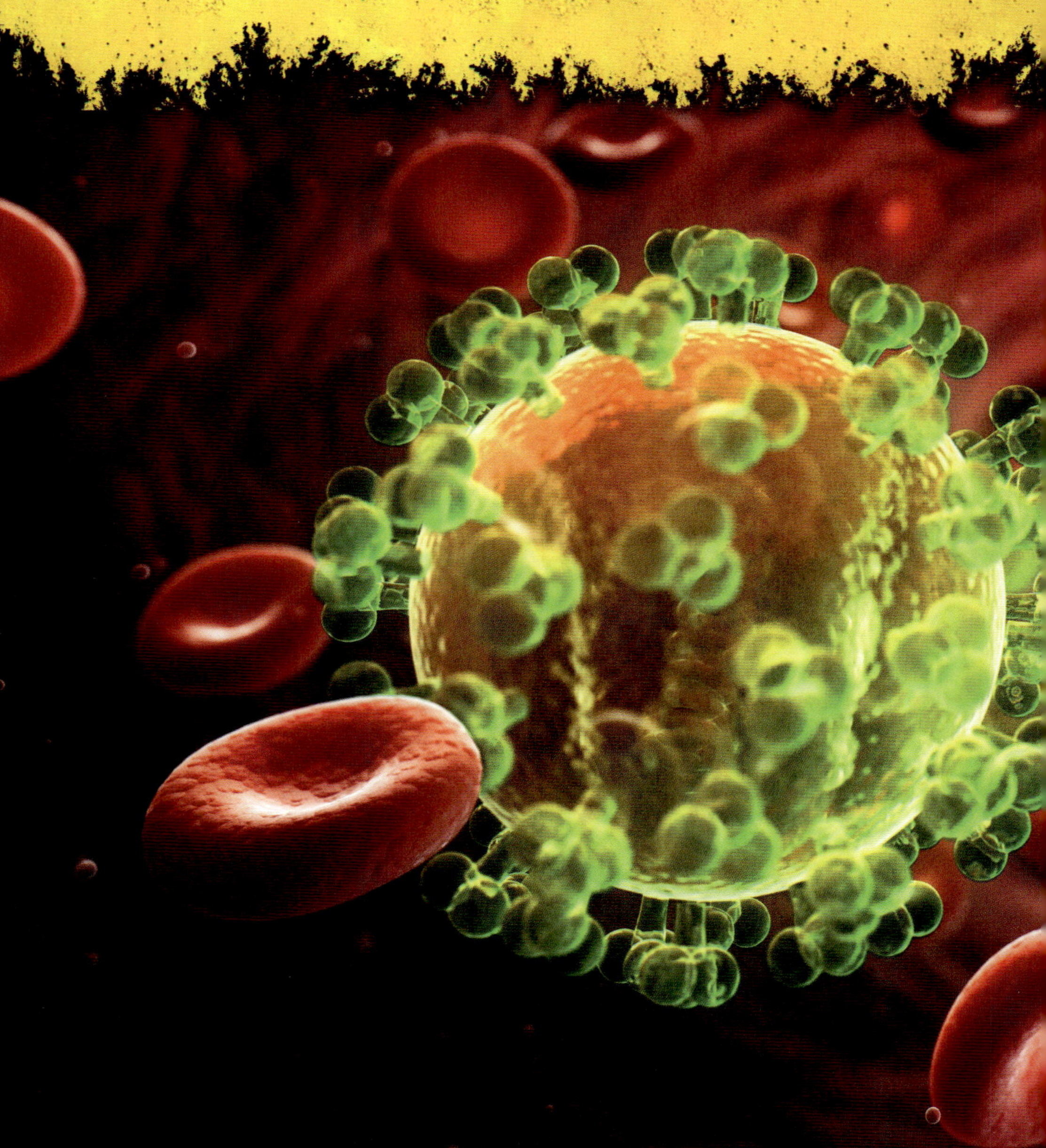

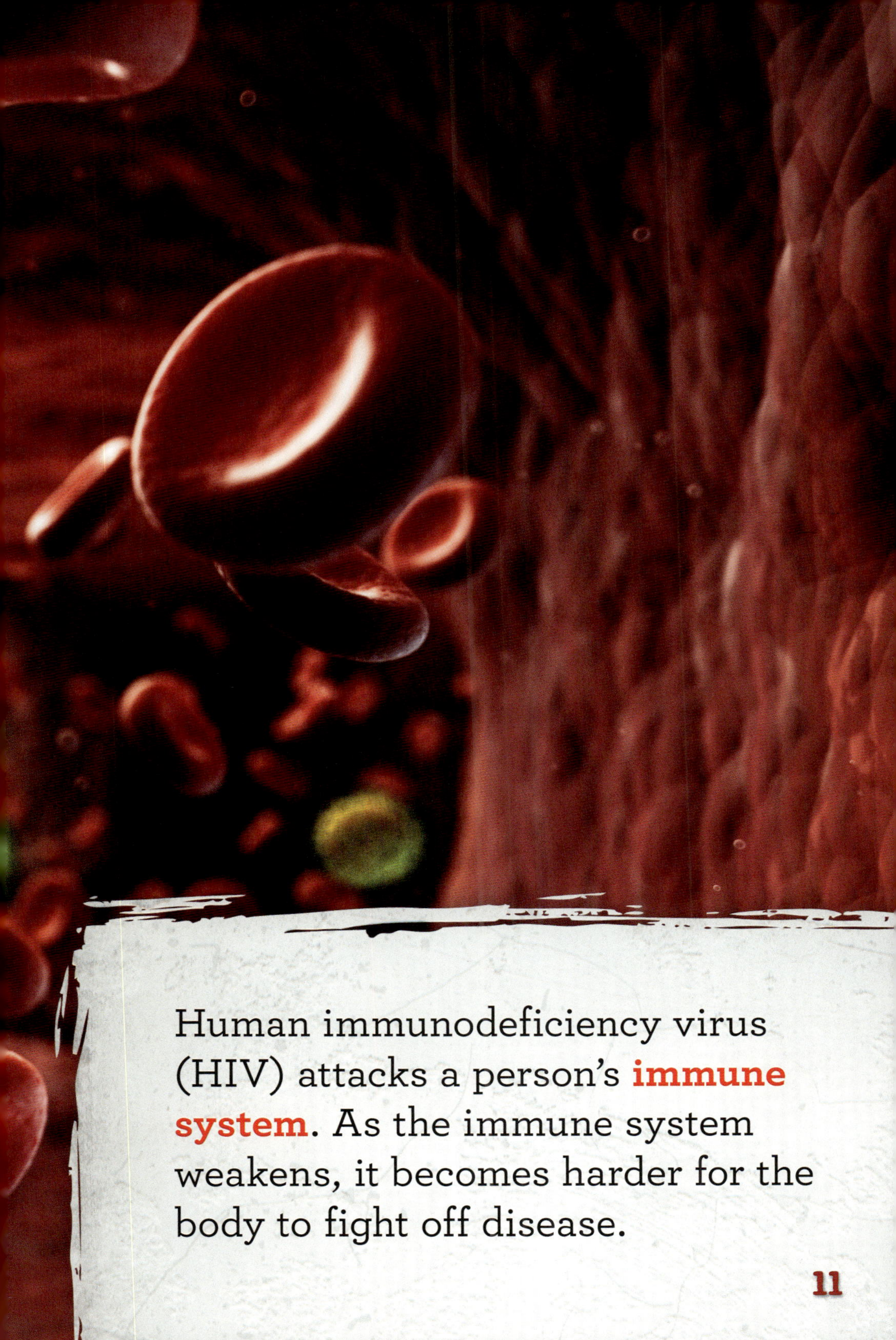

Human immunodeficiency virus (HIV) attacks a person's **immune system**. As the immune system weakens, it becomes harder for the body to fight off disease.

Acquired immunodeficiency syndrome (AIDS) is late stage HIV. It occurs when the body's **immune system** has been badly damaged by the virus.

OUTBREAK!

HIV is believed to have started around 1920 in the Democratic Republic of the Congo. It is there that scientists believe HIV **transferred** from apes to humans.

There were not many known cases until 1981. It was reported that five otherwise healthy men had become **infected**. The following year it had spread to 335 known people.

AIDS **activists** began to organize care for people who were ill. The Gay Men's Health Crisis was founded in 1982. It is the oldest HIV/AIDS service organization in the world.

In 1984, researchers discovered that HIV caused AIDS. By the end of 1985, there were more than 20,000 cases throughout the world.

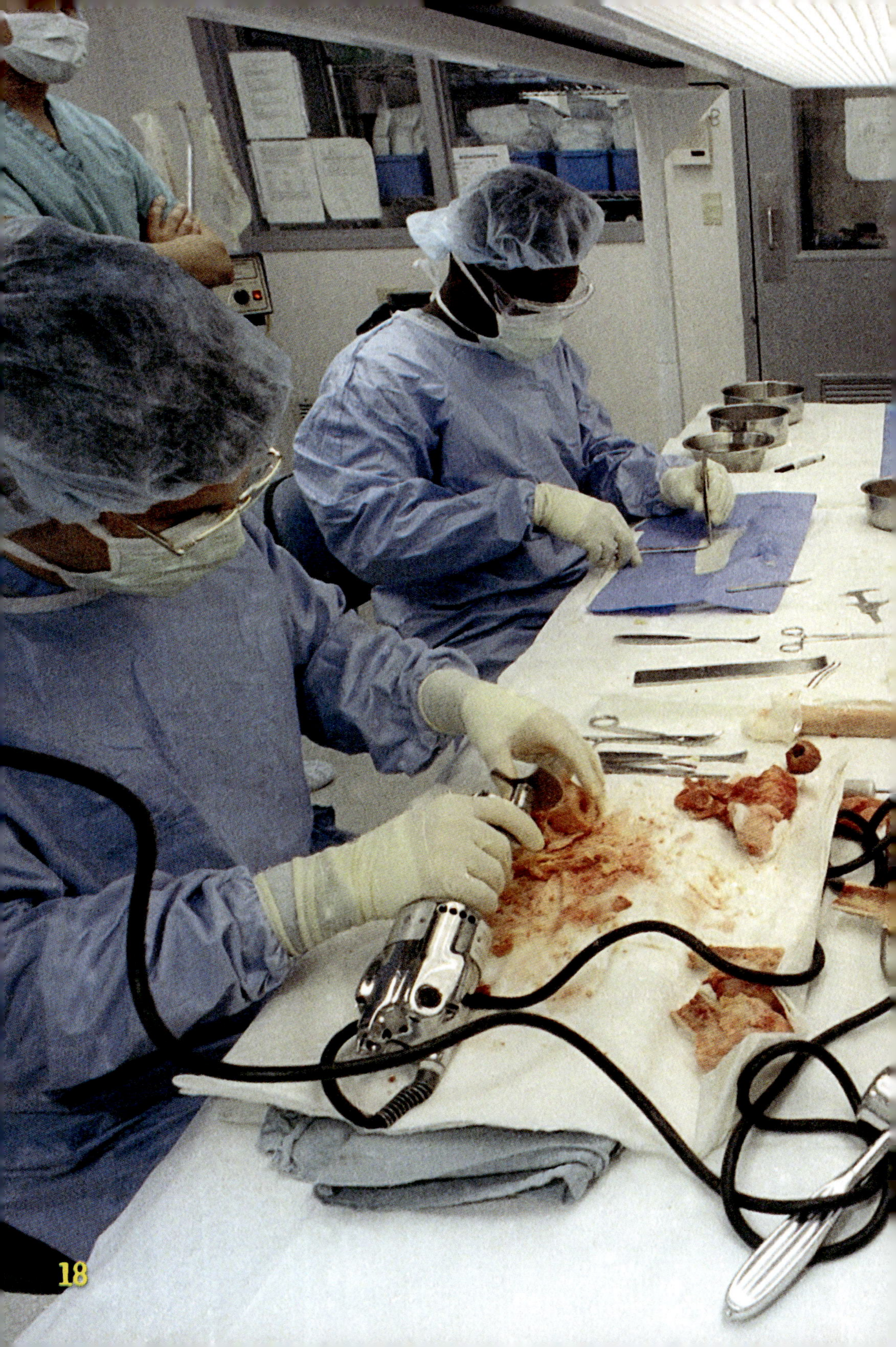

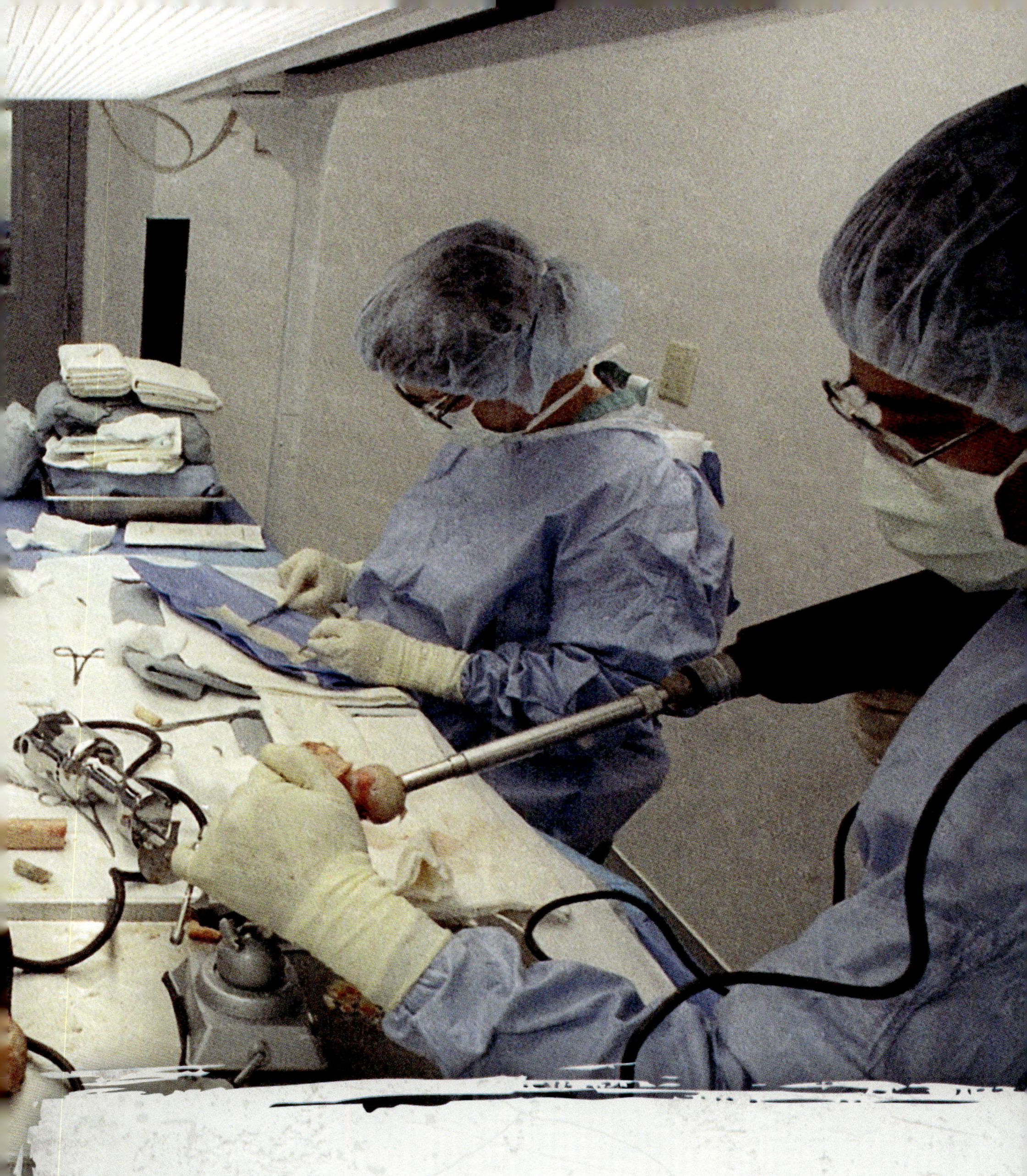

The first treatments for HIV became available in 1987. Deaths began to drop greatly in 1995 thanks to new medications and testing.

More than 74 million people have been **infected** with HIV. About 32 million have died from AIDS since the start of the **pandemic**.

Today, advanced testing and medication have helped people with HIV/AIDS live longer. AIDS-related deaths have been lowered by more than 50% since the peak in 2004.

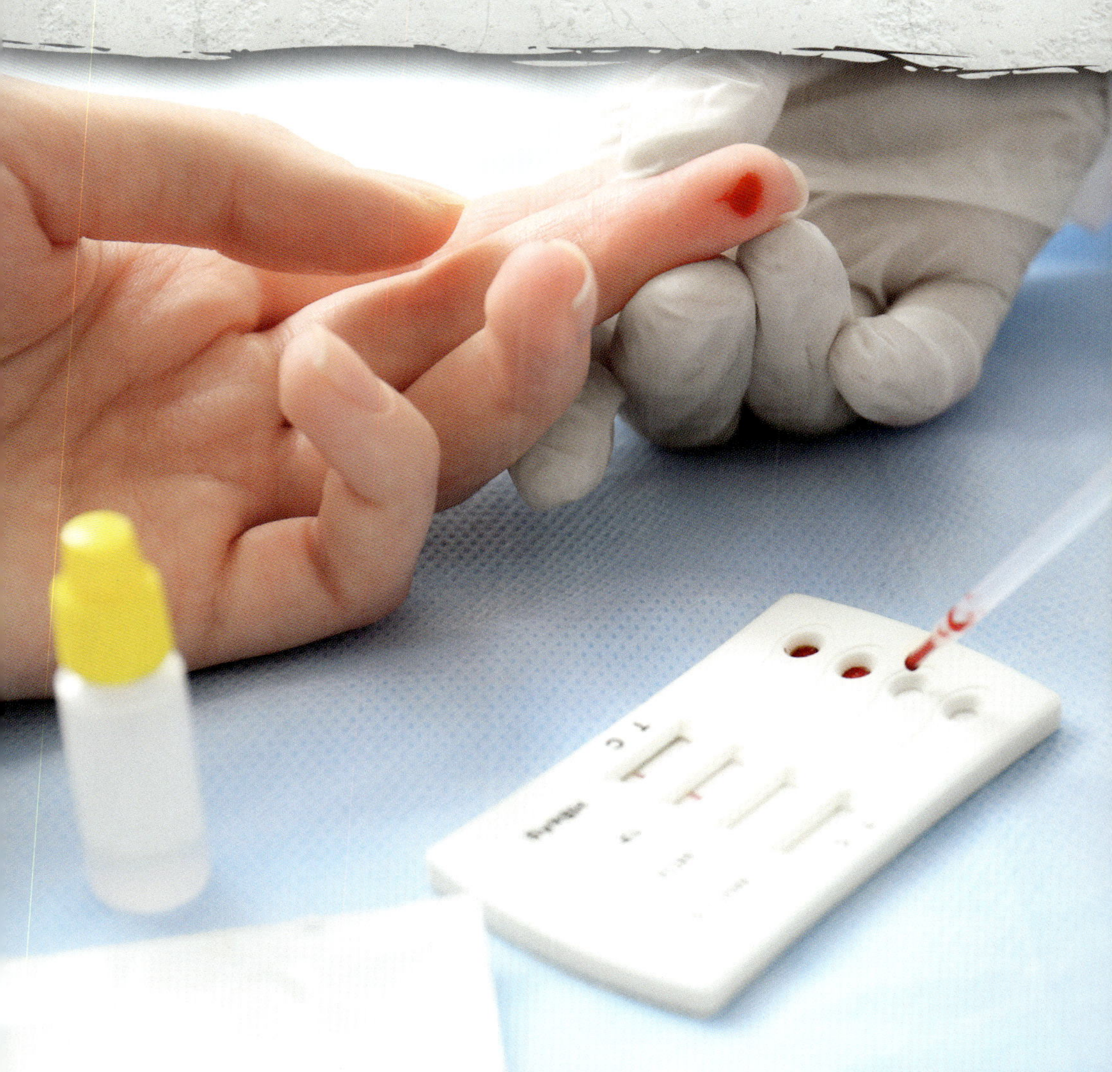

GLOSSARY

activist – one who fights for a cause.

immune system – the body's germ fighting system.

infect – to spread germs or disease to.

pandemic – a worldwide disease outbreak.

symptoms – the signs that a person is ill or is becoming sick.

transfer – the passing of a disease to someone or something else.

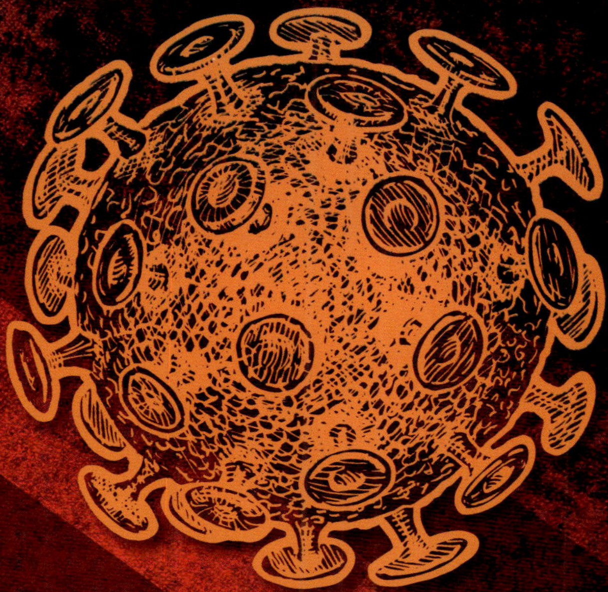

ONLINE RESOURCES

To learn more about the AIDS Crisis, please visit **abdobooklinks.com** or scan this QR code. These links are routinely monitored and updated to provide the most current information available.

INDEX